GEORGE

by Maggie Stern

illustrations by
Blanche Sims

ORCHARD BOOKS • NEW YORK

Orchard Books, A Grolier Company
95 Madison Avenue, New York, NY 10016

Manufactured in the United States of America
Printed and bound by Phoenix Color Corp.
Book design by Helene Berinsky
The text of this book is set in 18 point Goudy.
The illustrations are pen and ink with watercolor.

Hardcover 10 9 8 7 6 5 4 3 2 1
Paperback 10 9 8 7 6 5 4 3 2 1

Library of Congress Cataloging-in-Publication Data
Stern, Maggie.
George / by Maggie Stern ; illustrations by Blanche Sims.
p. cm.
Summary: At school George recovers an escaped rabbit, helps bake bread,
and enjoys a fair at which he hopes to win a raffle prize.
ISBN 0-531-30197-4 (trade : alk. paper)
ISBN 0-531-33197-0 (lib. bdg. : alk. paper)
ISBN 0-531-07135-9 (pbk. : alk. paper)
[1. Schools—Fiction.]   I. Sims, Blanche, ill.   II. Title.
PZ7.S83875Gg   1999
[Fic]—dc21   99-11665

For Susan and David, with love

—M.S.

To Zazie

—love Blanche

Contents

Pumpkin

Just before lunch, Mrs. Elton's class
had chore time.

George called out,

"Can I feed Pumpkin? Can I?"

He always wanted to be first.

"Shh," said Mrs. Elton.

"Who will carry the book orders

to the office?"

"Me!" shouted George.

Joey's arm shot up

straight as a pencil.

Mrs. Elton pointed to Joey.

"Now I need two students to write

today's weather report on the board."

"I will," called George.

Mrs. Elton pointed to James and Alice.

"Now I need someone to feed the rabbit."

"I asked first," said George,

bounding off his seat.

"George," said Mrs. Elton,

"remember rule #1: no calling out.

Be still and wait your turn.

Sarah, I would like you
to feed Pumpkin, please."
George sank down in his seat.
It was so hard to wait.
"Time for Pumpkin's lunch,"
said Sarah.
She opened the hutch door.

Pumpkin hopped from the cage
and out the classroom door!

"Pumpkin, stop!" called Mrs. Elton.

Pumpkin was not listening.

George dashed after him.

At the corner, Pumpkin
stopped and sniffed the air.
George dove at the rabbit,
but Pumpkin escaped
through a doorway.
Someone was playing the piano.
Pumpkin ran forward, then stopped.
He was on stage,
in front of twelve girls in tutus.

Pumpkin slipped out
through the stage door.

George chased Pumpkin into the library.

The rabbit knocked over a stack of books

and darted away again!

George ran past the principal.

"Excuse me, Mrs. Abbott," said George.

"Have you seen a rabbit?"

"He has not been sent to my office,"

said Mrs. Abbott.

She winked.

George checked
under seats in
the computer lab.
No Pumpkin.

He peeked in
the nurse's office.
No Pumpkin.

George heard a lot of noise
from the cafeteria.
He ran in.

His class was eating lunch.

"A rat!" a lunch lady shrieked.

"Call the police."

"Pumpkin is *not* a rat," George said.

"He is a rabbit."

"Grab him!" Howie shouted.

Pumpkin hid under the salad bar.

"Corner him," Joey said,

charging at the rabbit.

"Wait!" said George.

"You are scaring him."

Joey turned around and stared at George.

The lunch lady stopped screaming.

George spoke calmly.

"Everyone be still."

Slowly George tiptoed toward

the salad bar.

Pumpkin watched him.

George dipped his hand into a tray.

He picked up a

bright green leaf of lettuce.

No one moved.

They all watched George.

George held the lettuce in
front of Pumpkin.

Pumpkin edged closer.

His nose twitched.

When Pumpkin nibbled the lettuce,
George picked him up.

"Got you," he said.

"Well done, George!"
said Mrs. Elton.

"It is time to go back to class.

I will get you a sandwich."

George put Pumpkin into his cage.

Then he fed him the lettuce.

"See, George," said Mrs. Elton.

"Sometimes it is good to wait."

George took his seat quietly.

He ate his sandwich.

"It is time to line up for gym,"

said Mrs. Elton.

Smiling, George took his place.

At the end of the line.

The Secret Agent

It was project day at school.

"I am sick," George said.

"You will love cooking," said Mom.

His brother, Henry, snickered.

"Dullsville," said his sister, Lulu.

In the classroom, Mrs. Elton held
a bag of flour.
Then she held up
a small packet.
"Who knows what
yeast is?" she asked.
George threw himself on the floor.
"George, do you?"
George shook his head.
"We mix yeast with the flour,"
said Mrs. Elton.
"It is the agent that makes bread rise."

George sat up.

"You mean like a secret agent?"

"Exactly," said Mrs. Elton.

"Who will be my helper?"

George's hand shot up.

"Thank you, George," said Mrs. Elton.

"To bake bread, we use flour,

water, and yeast."

George mixed them all in a bowl.

What would this secret agent do?

George added more yeast.

He rolled the dough into a ball

and kneaded it.

"Okay, that is enough, George.

Now we will wait for it to rise,"

said Mrs. Elton.

Howie went over to the rabbit cage.

Joey went to the block area.

George stared at the bread.

Nothing happened.

He wondered where the

secret agent was.

In the reading corner, George
pretended to catch fly balls
and hit home runs.

Then, after reading
a book, he peeked
at the dough.

"LOOK!" he shouted. "It is growing.
It is huge! Soon it will be
as tall as me!"

28

Everyone raced to the table.

"WOW!" they shouted.

"Punch the dough down,"

said Mrs. Elton.

George punched it.

"Now we will put the dough in a pan
and go down to the cafeteria and
put it into the oven," said Mrs. Elton.
George licked his lips as Mrs. Elton
slid the loaf into the oven.
"We will have some outside time
while the bread bakes,"
said Mrs. Elton.

In the school yard, George could not

keep his eyes off his watch.

His stomach growled.

He peeked through the kitchen

window, but the clock inside was

just as slow as his watch.

"How many more minutes?" he asked.

"Patience," said Mrs. Elton.

George practiced pitching
and sliding into base.
Finally Mrs. Elton called the class
and brought them inside again.
She looked into the oven and
clapped her hands.
"Done!" she said.
"We can eat!" said George.

"No," said Mrs. Elton.
"We must let the
bread cool."
George spun like a top.
It was so hard to wait.

At last Mrs. Elton sliced
the bread into fifteen pieces.
George took a bite.
"Delicious!" he shouted.
"Three cheers
for the secret agent!"

The next morning, George stumbled
into the kitchen.

"Mom," he said, "I am sick!"

"But you have gym," said Mom.

She felt his forehead.

"You do feel warm.

You had better stay home."

"He is not sick," said Henry.

"Faker," said Lulu.

After Henry and Lulu got on the bus,

George checked the cupboards.

"Mom," he said,

"do we have any yeast?"

The Fair

Dad drove Henry, Lulu, and
George to the school fair.
"Here are fifteen tickets each," Dad said.
"Thanks," they said.
"I will pick you up in two hours,"
said Dad.

Henry showed George and Lulu
the list of things to do.
"For one ticket, I can
dunk a teacher!" he said.
"For two tickets," said Lulu,
"I can go into the haunted house."

"For three tickets, I get a chance
at the raffle," said George.
"First prize is two box seats
at a baseball game!"
"Meet back here in thirty minutes,"
said Henry.

George ran to the raffle table.

"The more you put in," said the man,

"the better your chances

of winning!"

George could almost taste

the hot dog he would eat at the game.

He could hear the crack of the bat

against the ball.

George handed in *all* his tickets.

The man gave him five red cards.
George carefully wrote his
name, address, and telephone
number on the cards.
He put them into the slot
in the big white box.
"Have a lot of people entered?"
George asked.
"Not yet," said the man.

Howie came over and read

the prize list.

"Crummy choices," muttered George.

Sarah marched over.

"Rip-off," said George.

Howie bought one chance.

"Waste of money," said George.

Henry and Lulu walked over.

"I dunked Mr. Neff five times,"
said Henry.
"I touched fake brains
in the haunted house!" said Lulu.
"And then threw darts.
Now we will play mini-golf."
Henry and Lulu dashed ahead.
George followed.

Henry and Lulu
picked their clubs
and hit the ball.
George watched.

Then Henry and Lulu bowled.
George watched
some more.

Then came the ringtoss.
George loved the ringtoss.
His fingers itched to play.

"I have one ticket left," said Lulu.

"Me too," said Henry.

"We can fish for candy."

George sighed.

Then he saw the man placing

his hand in the raffle box.

It was time to pick the winners.

George, Henry, and Lulu

went over to watch.

George's heart pounded.

"Two free movie passes," the man said,

"go to . . . Roberto."

"Phew," said George.

"A pair of goldfish . . . to Kim."

The man pulled out another name.

George held his breath.

"Now for first prize.

Two box seats

at a baseball game . . ."

George crossed his fingers.

". . . to Howie," exclaimed the man.

George's eyes filled with tears.

Henry pushed George.

"Time to go!" he said.

George wiped his eyes and turned

to walk away.

"Oh, I forgot one prize," said the man.

"Fifteen tickets for next year's fair."

He reached into the box.

"And the winner is . . . George."

"That is you!" said Henry.

George looked up.

"That is me!" he shouted.

George took the tickets

and held them up.

"I know just how to use them," he said.

"Ten tickets for the raffle, and

five to dunk teachers!"

George raced to the car and hopped
into the front seat.

"How many more days until
next year's fair?" he asked.